50 Delicious Ramen Noodle Dishes from Japan

By: Kelly Johnson

Table of Contents

- Shoyu Ramen
- Miso Ramen
- Shio Ramen
- Tonkotsu Ramen
- Tsukemen
- Hiyashi Chuka
- Mazemen
- Yaki Ramen
- Hakata Ramen
- Sapporo Miso Ramen
- Kyoto-style Ramen
- Spicy Miso Ramen
- Ramen with Chashu Pork
- Seafood Ramen
- Ramen with Corn and Butter
- Ramen with Tofu
- Ramen with Soft-Boiled Egg
- Kimchi Ramen
- Curry Ramen

- Ramen with Bamboo Shoots
- Tan Tan Men
- Ramen with Nori (Seaweed)
- Spicy Kara Miso Ramen
- Wonton Ramen
- Ramen with Shiitake Mushrooms
- Ramen with Pickled Ginger
- Beef Ramen
- Ramen with Broccoli
- Vegetarian Ramen
- Ramen with Daikon
- Ramen with Sweet Potato
- Shoyu Tonkotsu Ramen
- Ramen with Spicy Chili Oil
- Paitan Ramen
- Miso and Garlic Ramen
- Ramen with Tempura Shrimp
- Ramen with Kimchi and Pork Belly
- Black Garlic Ramen
- Ramen with Tsukune (Chicken Meatballs)
- Ramen with Fried Tofu

- Ramen with Sweet Soy Sauce
- Ramen with Grilled Eel
- Ramen with Ramen Eggs
- Chilli Crab Ramen
- Pork and Gyoza Ramen
- Sumo Ramen
- Ramen with Sesame Paste
- Ramen with Spinach
- Chicken Karaage Ramen
- Ramen with Hot Sesame Oil

Shoyu Ramen

Ingredients:

- **For the broth:**
    - 4 cups chicken stock
    - 2 cups dashi stock
    - 1/4 cup soy sauce
    - 2 tbsp mirin
    - 1 tbsp sake
    - 1 tbsp sugar
    - 1 clove garlic, smashed
    - 1-inch piece of ginger, sliced
- **For the toppings:**
    - 2 soft-boiled eggs
    - 1/2 cup sliced green onions
    - 1/4 cup bamboo shoots
    - 1/4 cup nori (seaweed)
    - 2 slices of chashu pork
    - Ramen noodles

Instructions:

1. **Prepare the broth:** In a large pot, combine the chicken stock, dashi, soy sauce, mirin, sake, sugar, garlic, and ginger. Bring to a simmer and cook for **20-30 minutes**.
2. **Prepare the noodles:** Cook the ramen noodles according to package instructions. Drain and set aside.

3. **Assemble the ramen:** In bowls, place the cooked noodles and pour the hot broth over them.

4. **Top the ramen:** Add the soft-boiled eggs, green onions, bamboo shoots, nori, and chashu pork. Serve immediately.

Miso Ramen

Ingredients:

- **For the broth:**
    - 4 cups chicken stock
    - 2 cups dashi stock
    - 3 tbsp miso paste (preferably red miso)
    - 1 tbsp soy sauce
    - 1 tbsp sesame oil
    - 1 tbsp mirin
    - 1-inch piece of ginger, sliced
    - 1 clove garlic, smashed

- **For the toppings:**
    - 2 soft-boiled eggs
    - 1/2 cup corn
    - 1/4 cup green onions, sliced
    - 2 slices chashu pork
    - Ramen noodles

Instructions:

1. **Prepare the broth:** In a pot, heat the sesame oil and sauté the garlic and ginger for **1-2 minutes**. Add the chicken stock, dashi stock, miso paste, soy sauce, and mirin. Stir to dissolve the miso paste and bring to a simmer. Cook for **15-20 minutes**.

2. **Prepare the noodles:** Cook the ramen noodles according to package instructions. Drain and set aside.

3. **Assemble the ramen:** In bowls, place the cooked noodles and pour the miso broth over them.

4. **Top the ramen:** Add soft-boiled eggs, corn, green onions, and chashu pork. Serve immediately.

Shio Ramen

Ingredients:

- **For the broth:**
    - 4 cups chicken stock
    - 2 cups dashi stock
    - 1 tbsp sea salt (shio)
    - 1 tbsp soy sauce
    - 1 tbsp sake
    - 1 tbsp mirin
    - 1-inch piece of ginger, sliced
    - 1 clove garlic, smashed
- **For the toppings:**
    - 2 soft-boiled eggs
    - 1/2 cup sliced green onions
    - 1/4 cup nori
    - 2 slices of chashu pork
    - Ramen noodles

Instructions:

1. **Prepare the broth:** Combine the chicken stock, dashi stock, sea salt, soy sauce, sake, mirin, garlic, and ginger in a pot. Bring to a simmer and cook for **20-30 minutes**.
2. **Prepare the noodles:** Cook the ramen noodles according to package instructions. Drain and set aside.
3. **Assemble the ramen:** Place the noodles in bowls and pour the hot broth over them.

4. **Top the ramen:** Add the soft-boiled eggs, green onions, nori, and chashu pork. Serve immediately.

Tonkotsu Ramen

Ingredients:

- **For the broth:**
    - 4 cups pork stock
    - 1 cup chicken stock
    - 3 tbsp soy sauce
    - 1 tbsp mirin
    - 2 tbsp sesame oil
    - 1-inch piece of ginger, sliced
    - 2 cloves garlic, smashed
- **For the toppings:**
    - 2 soft-boiled eggs
    - 1/4 cup sliced green onions
    - 2 slices chashu pork
    - Ramen noodles

Instructions:

1. **Prepare the broth:** In a pot, combine the pork stock, chicken stock, soy sauce, mirin, sesame oil, garlic, and ginger. Bring to a simmer and cook for **30-45 minutes**.
2. **Prepare the noodles:** Cook the ramen noodles according to package instructions. Drain and set aside.
3. **Assemble the ramen:** Place the noodles in bowls and pour the tonkotsu broth over them.
4. **Top the ramen:** Add the soft-boiled eggs, green onions, and chashu pork. Serve immediately.

Tsukemen (Dipping Ramen)

Ingredients:

- **For the dipping sauce:**
    - 2 cups chicken stock
    - 1/4 cup soy sauce
    - 1 tbsp mirin
    - 1 tbsp sesame oil
    - 1-inch piece of ginger, sliced
    - 1 clove garlic, smashed
- **For the noodles and toppings:**
    - Ramen noodles (for dipping)
    - 2 soft-boiled eggs
    - 1/4 cup sliced green onions
    - 2 slices of chashu pork
    - Nori sheets

Instructions:

1. **Prepare the dipping sauce:** In a pot, combine the chicken stock, soy sauce, mirin, sesame oil, garlic, and ginger. Bring to a simmer and cook for **10-15 minutes**.

2. **Prepare the noodles:** Cook the ramen noodles according to package instructions. Drain and set aside.

3. **Assemble the tsukemen:** Serve the noodles on a plate alongside the dipping sauce in a small bowl.

4. **Top the noodles:** Add the soft-boiled eggs, green onions, chashu pork, and nori to the noodles. Dip the noodles into the sauce and enjoy.

Hiyashi Chuka (Cold Ramen)

Ingredients:

- 4 cups chicken broth
- 2 tbsp soy sauce
- 1 tbsp rice vinegar
- 1 tbsp sesame oil
- 1 tbsp sugar
- Ramen noodles (chilled)
- 2 slices of cucumber, julienned
- 2 slices of ham or chashu pork, thinly sliced
- 1/4 cup shredded egg (scrambled and cooked)
- 1/4 cup sliced green onions
- 1/4 tsp sesame seeds

Instructions:

1. **Prepare the sauce:** In a bowl, combine the chicken broth, soy sauce, rice vinegar, sesame oil, and sugar. Mix until the sugar dissolves.

2. **Prepare the noodles:** Cook the ramen noodles, then cool them under cold running water and set aside.

3. **Assemble the dish:** Place the chilled noodles in a bowl and pour the sauce over them.

4. **Top the ramen:** Add the cucumber, ham or chashu pork, scrambled egg, green onions, and sesame seeds. Serve cold.

Mazemen

Ingredients:

- **For the sauce:**
    - 2 tbsp soy sauce
    - 1 tbsp sesame oil
    - 1 tbsp rice vinegar
    - 1 tbsp sugar
    - 1 tsp chili oil (optional)
- **For the noodles and toppings:**
    - Ramen noodles
    - 2 soft-boiled eggs
    - 1/4 cup sliced green onions
    - 1/4 cup shredded nori
    - 2 slices of chashu pork

Instructions:

1. **Prepare the sauce:** In a small bowl, combine the soy sauce, sesame oil, rice vinegar, sugar, and chili oil (if using). Stir until the sugar dissolves.
2. **Prepare the noodles:** Cook the ramen noodles according to package instructions. Drain and set aside.
3. **Assemble the mazemen:** Toss the noodles with the sauce in a bowl.
4. **Top the ramen:** Add the soft-boiled eggs, green onions, shredded nori, and chashu pork. Serve immediately.

Yaki Ramen (Grilled Ramen)

Ingredients:

- Ramen noodles
- 2 tbsp soy sauce
- 1 tbsp sesame oil
- 1 tsp mirin
- 1/4 cup sliced mushrooms
- 1/4 cup sliced green onions
- 1/4 cup cooked chicken or pork, sliced
- 1 tbsp sesame seeds

Instructions:

1. **Prepare the noodles:** Cook the ramen noodles and drain them.
2. **Grill the noodles:** Heat sesame oil in a pan over medium-high heat. Add the noodles and stir-fry for about **3-4 minutes** until slightly crispy.
3. **Assemble the dish:** Add the soy sauce, mirin, mushrooms, green onions, and cooked meat. Stir-fry for another **1-2 minutes**.
4. **Top the ramen:** Sprinkle with sesame seeds and serve.

Hakata Ramen

Ingredients:

- **For the broth:**
    - 4 cups pork stock
    - 1 cup chicken stock
    - 2 tbsp soy sauce
    - 1 tbsp mirin
    - 2 tbsp sesame oil
    - 1-inch piece of ginger, sliced
    - 2 cloves garlic, smashed
- **For the toppings:**
    - 2 soft-boiled eggs
    - 1/4 cup sliced green onions
    - 2 slices chashu pork
    - Ramen noodles

Instructions:

1. **Prepare the broth:** In a pot, combine the pork stock, chicken stock, soy sauce, mirin, sesame oil, garlic, and ginger. Bring to a simmer and cook for **30-45 minutes**.
2. **Prepare the noodles:** Cook the ramen noodles according to package instructions. Drain and set aside.
3. **Assemble the ramen:** Place the noodles in bowls and pour the Hakata broth over them.
4. **Top the ramen:** Add the soft-boiled eggs, green onions, and chashu pork. Serve immediately.

Sapporo Miso Ramen

Ingredients:

- **For the broth:**
    - 4 cups chicken stock
    - 2 cups miso paste
    - 1 tbsp soy sauce
    - 1 tbsp sesame oil
    - 1 tbsp mirin
    - 1-inch piece of ginger, sliced
    - 2 cloves garlic, smashed
- **For the toppings:**
    - 2 soft-boiled eggs
    - 1/4 cup corn
    - 1/4 cup sliced green onions
    - 2 slices chashu pork
    - Ramen noodles

Instructions:

1. **Prepare the broth:** In a pot, heat the sesame oil and sauté garlic and ginger for **1-2 minutes**. Add the chicken stock, miso paste, soy sauce, and mirin. Bring to a simmer and cook for **20-30 minutes**.
2. **Prepare the noodles:** Cook the ramen noodles according to package instructions. Drain and set aside.
3. **Assemble the ramen:** In bowls, place the cooked noodles and pour the miso broth over them.

4. **Top the ramen:** Add soft-boiled eggs, corn, green onions, and chashu pork. Serve immediately.

Kyoto-Style Ramen

(Known for a richer, slightly sweet soy-based broth)

Ingredients:

- **For the broth:**
    - 4 cups chicken stock
    - 2 cups dashi stock
    - 1/4 cup soy sauce
    - 2 tbsp mirin
    - 1 tbsp sake
    - 1 tbsp sugar
    - 1 tbsp sesame oil
    - 1-inch piece of ginger, sliced
    - 1 clove garlic, smashed
- **For the toppings:**
    - 2 soft-boiled eggs
    - 2 slices of chashu pork
    - 1/4 cup green onions, sliced
    - 1/4 cup bamboo shoots
    - Ramen noodles

Instructions:

1. **Prepare the broth:** Combine chicken stock, dashi, soy sauce, mirin, sake, sugar, sesame oil, ginger, and garlic in a pot. Simmer for **20-30 minutes**.

2. **Prepare the noodles:** Cook ramen noodles according to package instructions.

3. **Assemble the ramen:** Divide the noodles into bowls and pour the hot broth over them.

4. **Top the ramen:** Add soft-boiled eggs, chashu pork, green onions, and bamboo shoots.

Spicy Miso Ramen

Ingredients:

- **For the broth:**
    - 4 cups chicken stock
    - 2 tbsp miso paste (red miso for extra heat)
    - 1 tbsp soy sauce
    - 1 tbsp chili paste (or 1 tsp chili oil for a milder version)
    - 1 tbsp mirin
    - 1-inch piece of ginger, minced
    - 1 clove garlic, minced
- **For the toppings:**
    - 2 slices chashu pork
    - 1/4 cup bean sprouts
    - 1/4 cup corn
    - 1 soft-boiled egg
    - 1 tbsp sesame seeds
    - Ramen noodles

Instructions:

1. **Prepare the broth:** Heat sesame oil in a pot and sauté garlic, ginger, and chili paste. Add chicken stock, miso paste, soy sauce, and mirin. Simmer for **15-20 minutes**.
2. **Prepare the noodles:** Cook ramen noodles and set aside.
3. **Assemble the ramen:** Pour the broth over the noodles in a bowl.

4. **Top the ramen:** Add chashu pork, bean sprouts, corn, soft-boiled egg, and sesame seeds.

Ramen with Chashu Pork

Ingredients:

- **For the broth:**
    - 4 cups pork stock
    - 2 tbsp soy sauce
    - 1 tbsp mirin
    - 1 tbsp sake
    - 1-inch piece of ginger, sliced
- **For the toppings:**
    - 3 slices homemade chashu pork (see instructions below)
    - 1/4 cup sliced green onions
    - 1 soft-boiled egg
    - 1 sheet of nori
    - Ramen noodles

Instructions:

1. **Prepare the broth:** Simmer pork stock, soy sauce, mirin, sake, and ginger for **30 minutes**.
2. **Prepare the chashu pork:**
    - Roll a pork belly slab and tie with kitchen twine.
    - Sear all sides in a pan.
    - Simmer in a mix of soy sauce, mirin, sake, garlic, and ginger for **90 minutes**.
    - Cool and slice thinly.

3. **Prepare the noodles:** Cook and drain ramen noodles.

4. **Assemble the ramen:** Pour broth over the noodles and add chashu pork, green onions, and nori.

Seafood Ramen

Ingredients:

- **For the broth:**
    - 4 cups seafood stock (or dashi + shrimp shells boiled in water)
    - 2 tbsp miso paste
    - 1 tbsp soy sauce
    - 1 tbsp mirin
- **For the toppings:**
    - 4 shrimp, peeled
    - 1/4 cup squid rings
    - 1 soft-boiled egg
    - 1/4 cup sliced green onions
    - Ramen noodles

Instructions:

1. **Prepare the broth:** Simmer seafood stock with miso, soy sauce, and mirin for **15 minutes**.
2. **Prepare the seafood:** Sauté shrimp and squid rings in sesame oil.
3. **Prepare the noodles:** Cook and drain ramen noodles.
4. **Assemble the ramen:** Pour broth over the noodles and add seafood, green onions, and egg.

Ramen with Corn and Butter

Ingredients:

- **For the broth:**
    - 4 cups chicken stock
    - 2 tbsp miso paste
    - 1 tbsp soy sauce
    - 1 tbsp mirin
- **For the toppings:**
    - 1/2 cup corn kernels
    - 1 tbsp unsalted butter
    - 1/4 cup sliced green onions
    - Ramen noodles

Instructions:

1. **Prepare the broth:** Simmer chicken stock, miso, soy sauce, and mirin for **15-20 minutes**.
2. **Prepare the noodles:** Cook and drain ramen noodles.
3. **Assemble the ramen:** Pour broth over the noodles, top with corn and a pat of butter, and let it melt.

Ramen with Tofu

Ingredients:

- **For the broth:**
    - 4 cups vegetable stock
    - 2 tbsp miso paste
    - 1 tbsp soy sauce
- **For the toppings:**
    - 1/2 cup cubed firm tofu
    - 1/4 cup sliced green onions
    - Ramen noodles

Instructions:

1. **Prepare the broth:** Simmer vegetable stock, miso, and soy sauce for **15 minutes**.
2. **Prepare the tofu:** Lightly pan-fry or serve raw.
3. **Assemble the ramen:** Pour broth over the noodles and add tofu and green onions.

Ramen with Soft-Boiled Egg

Use any broth, but ensure the egg is cooked for **6 minutes**, then chilled and peeled for a gooey yolk.

Kimchi Ramen

Ingredients:

- **For the broth:**
    - 4 cups chicken or pork stock
    - 1/2 cup chopped kimchi
    - 1 tbsp gochujang (Korean chili paste)
    - 1 tbsp soy sauce
- **For the toppings:**
    - 1/4 cup sliced green onions
    - 1/2 cup more kimchi
    - 1 soft-boiled egg
    - Ramen noodles

Instructions:

1. **Prepare the broth:** Simmer stock with kimchi, gochujang, and soy sauce for **15-20 minutes**.
2. **Prepare the noodles:** Cook and drain ramen noodles.
3. **Assemble the ramen:** Pour broth over the noodles and top with extra kimchi, green onions, and egg.

Curry Ramen

Ingredients:

- **For the broth:**
    - 4 cups chicken stock
    - 1 tbsp curry powder
    - 1 tbsp miso paste
    - 1 tbsp soy sauce
- **For the toppings:**
    - 1/4 cup shredded carrots
    - 1/4 cup green onions
    - 2 slices chashu pork
    - Ramen noodles

Instructions:

1. **Prepare the broth:** Simmer stock with curry powder, miso, and soy sauce for **15 minutes**.
2. **Prepare the noodles:** Cook and drain ramen noodles.
3. **Assemble the ramen:** Pour broth over the noodles and add carrots, green onions, and pork.

Ramen with Bamboo Shoots

Use any broth and add **1/4 cup menma (fermented bamboo shoots)** as a topping.

Tan Tan Men (Spicy Sesame Ramen)

(A Japanese take on Sichuan Dan Dan noodles, with a rich, spicy, and nutty broth)

Ingredients:

- **For the broth:**
    - 4 cups chicken or vegetable stock
    - 2 tbsp sesame paste (or tahini)
    - 1 tbsp miso paste
    - 1 tbsp soy sauce
    - 1 tbsp sake
    - 1 tbsp chili oil
    - 1 tsp ground Sichuan peppercorns (optional, for numbing spice)
- **For the toppings:**
    - 1/2 cup ground pork (or tofu for a vegetarian option)
    - 1 clove garlic, minced
    - 1 tsp ginger, minced
    - 1 tbsp soy sauce
    - 1 tsp sesame oil
    - 1/4 cup chopped green onions
    - 1 soft-boiled egg
    - Ramen noodles

Instructions:

1. **Prepare the broth:** In a pot, whisk together stock, sesame paste, miso, soy sauce, sake, chili oil, and Sichuan pepper. Simmer for **15 minutes**.

2. **Prepare the pork or tofu:** In a pan, cook ground pork (or tofu) with garlic, ginger, soy sauce, and sesame oil until browned.

3. **Prepare the noodles:** Cook and drain ramen noodles.

4. **Assemble the ramen:** Pour broth over noodles and top with pork, green onions, and a soft-boiled egg.

Ramen with Nori (Seaweed)

(A simple, umami-rich ramen with seaweed flavor)

Ingredients:

- **For the broth:**
    - 4 cups dashi stock (or chicken stock with kombu)
    - 1 tbsp soy sauce
    - 1 tbsp mirin
    - 1 tbsp miso paste
- **For the toppings:**
    - 2 sheets nori (toasted seaweed), torn or whole
    - 1/4 cup sliced green onions
    - 1 soft-boiled egg
    - Ramen noodles

Instructions:

1. **Prepare the broth:** Simmer dashi stock with soy sauce, mirin, and miso for **15 minutes**.
2. **Prepare the noodles:** Cook and drain ramen noodles.
3. **Assemble the ramen:** Pour broth over noodles and top with nori, green onions, and a soft-boiled egg.

Spicy Kara Miso Ramen

(A Sapporo-style ramen with a spicy miso blend)

Ingredients:

- **For the broth:**
    - 4 cups pork or chicken stock
    - 2 tbsp red miso paste
    - 1 tbsp soy sauce
    - 1 tbsp sake
    - 1 tbsp chili paste (or chili oil)
    - 1 tsp grated garlic
    - 1 tsp grated ginger
- **For the toppings:**
    - 1/2 cup bean sprouts
    - 2 slices chashu pork
    - 1 tbsp butter (for richness)
    - 1 soft-boiled egg
    - Ramen noodles

Instructions:

1. **Prepare the broth:** Simmer stock with miso, soy sauce, sake, chili paste, garlic, and ginger for **20 minutes**.
2. **Prepare the noodles:** Cook and drain ramen noodles.
3. **Assemble the ramen:** Pour broth over noodles, add toppings, and finish with butter for a rich taste.

Wonton Ramen

(A fusion of Japanese ramen and Chinese wonton soup)

Ingredients:

- **For the broth:**
    - 4 cups chicken stock
    - 1 tbsp soy sauce
    - 1 tbsp mirin
    - 1 tsp grated ginger
- **For the wontons:**
    - 10 wonton wrappers
    - 1/2 cup ground pork (or shrimp)
    - 1 clove garlic, minced
    - 1 tsp soy sauce
    - 1/2 tsp sesame oil
- **For the toppings:**
    - 1/4 cup chopped green onions
    - 1 soft-boiled egg
    - Ramen noodles

Instructions:

1. **Prepare the broth:** Simmer chicken stock with soy sauce, mirin, and ginger for **15 minutes**.
2. **Prepare the wontons:** Mix pork, garlic, soy sauce, and sesame oil. Place a small amount in each wonton wrapper, fold, and seal. Boil for **3-4 minutes**.

3. **Prepare the noodles:** Cook and drain ramen noodles.

4. **Assemble the ramen:** Pour broth over noodles and add wontons and toppings.

Ramen with Shiitake Mushrooms

Ingredients:

- **For the broth:**
    - 4 cups vegetable or chicken stock
    - 1 tbsp soy sauce
    - 1 tbsp mirin
    - 1/2 cup sliced shiitake mushrooms
- **For the toppings:**
    - 1/4 cup green onions
    - 1 soft-boiled egg
    - 1 sheet nori
    - Ramen noodles

Instructions:

1. **Prepare the broth:** Simmer stock with soy sauce, mirin, and shiitake mushrooms for **15 minutes**.
2. **Prepare the noodles:** Cook and drain ramen noodles.
3. **Assemble the ramen:** Pour broth over noodles and top with mushrooms and other toppings.

Ramen with Pickled Ginger

Simply add **1-2 tbsp of pickled ginger (beni shoga)** as a topping to any ramen for a tangy flavor boost.

Beef Ramen

Ingredients:

- **For the broth:**
    - 4 cups beef stock
    - 1 tbsp soy sauce
    - 1 tbsp miso paste
- **For the toppings:**
    - 1/2 cup thinly sliced beef (such as ribeye)
    - 1/4 cup sliced green onions
    - 1 soft-boiled egg
    - Ramen noodles

Instructions:

1. **Prepare the broth:** Simmer beef stock, soy sauce, and miso for **15 minutes**.
2. **Prepare the beef:** Sear thinly sliced beef in a pan for **1-2 minutes**.
3. **Assemble the ramen:** Pour broth over noodles and add beef and toppings.

Ramen with Broccoli

Simply add **1/2 cup steamed or stir-fried broccoli** as a topping for a nutritious addition.

Vegetarian Ramen

Ingredients:

- **For the broth:**
    - 4 cups vegetable stock
    - 1 tbsp miso paste
    - 1 tbsp soy sauce
    - 1 tsp sesame oil
- **For the toppings:**
    - 1/4 cup steamed spinach
    - 1/4 cup corn
    - 1/2 cup tofu, cubed
    - 1/4 cup sliced green onions
    - Ramen noodles

Instructions:

1. **Prepare the broth:** Simmer vegetable stock, miso paste, soy sauce, and sesame oil for **15 minutes**.
2. **Prepare the noodles:** Cook and drain ramen noodles.
3. **Assemble the ramen:** Pour broth over noodles and add vegetarian toppings.

Ramen with Daikon

(A light and refreshing ramen with daikon's mild sweetness)

Ingredients:

- **For the broth:**
    - 4 cups dashi stock (or chicken stock)
    - 1 tbsp soy sauce
    - 1 tbsp mirin
    - 1/2 cup thinly sliced daikon radish
- **For the toppings:**
    - 1/4 cup sliced green onions
    - 1 soft-boiled egg
    - Ramen noodles

Instructions:

1. **Prepare the broth:** Simmer dashi stock, soy sauce, mirin, and daikon slices for **15 minutes** until daikon is tender.
2. **Prepare the noodles:** Cook and drain ramen noodles.
3. **Assemble the ramen:** Pour broth over noodles and top with daikon and other toppings.

Ramen with Sweet Potato

(A slightly sweet and creamy ramen with roasted sweet potatoes)

Ingredients:

- **For the broth:**
    - 4 cups vegetable or chicken stock
    - 1 tbsp soy sauce
    - 1 tbsp miso paste
    - 1/2 cup mashed roasted sweet potato
- **For the toppings:**
    - 1/4 cup cubed roasted sweet potatoes
    - 1/4 cup spinach
    - 1 soft-boiled egg
    - Ramen noodles

Instructions:

1. **Prepare the broth:** Blend roasted sweet potato into the stock with miso and soy sauce. Simmer for **15 minutes**.
2. **Prepare the noodles:** Cook and drain ramen noodles.
3. **Assemble the ramen:** Pour broth over noodles and add toppings.

Shoyu Tonkotsu Ramen

(A rich tonkotsu broth with a soy sauce base)

Ingredients:

- **For the broth:**
    - 6 cups tonkotsu broth (pork bone broth, simmered for 12+ hours)
    - 2 tbsp soy sauce
    - 1 tbsp mirin
    - 1 tbsp sake
- **For the toppings:**
    - 2 slices chashu pork
    - 1 soft-boiled egg
    - 1 sheet nori
    - 1/4 cup sliced green onions
    - Ramen noodles

Instructions:

1. **Prepare the broth:** Mix tonkotsu broth with soy sauce, mirin, and sake. Simmer for **10 minutes**.
2. **Prepare the noodles:** Cook and drain ramen noodles.
3. **Assemble the ramen:** Pour broth over noodles and top with chashu, egg, and nori.

Ramen with Spicy Chili Oil

(A fiery ramen with bold heat)

Ingredients:

- **For the broth:**
    - 4 cups chicken stock
    - 1 tbsp miso paste
    - 1 tbsp soy sauce
    - 1 tbsp chili oil
- **For the toppings:**
    - 1/4 cup bean sprouts
    - 1 tbsp extra chili oil
    - 1/4 cup sliced green onions
    - Ramen noodles

Instructions:

1. **Prepare the broth:** Simmer stock with miso, soy sauce, and chili oil for **10 minutes**.
2. **Prepare the noodles:** Cook and drain ramen noodles.
3. **Assemble the ramen:** Pour broth over noodles, add toppings, and drizzle more chili oil.

Paitan Ramen

(A creamy, milky chicken-based ramen)

Ingredients:

- **For the broth:**
    - 6 cups chicken stock (simmered with chicken bones for a milky texture)
    - 1 tbsp soy sauce
    - 1 tbsp miso paste
- **For the toppings:**
    - 1/2 cup shredded chicken
    - 1/4 cup corn
    - 1 soft-boiled egg
    - Ramen noodles

Instructions:

1. **Prepare the broth:** Simmer chicken stock until cloudy. Mix in soy sauce and miso.
2. **Prepare the noodles:** Cook and drain ramen noodles.
3. **Assemble the ramen:** Pour broth over noodles and add toppings.

Miso and Garlic Ramen

(A deeply umami miso ramen with roasted garlic)

Ingredients:

- **For the broth:**
    - 4 cups chicken stock
    - 2 tbsp miso paste
    - 1 tbsp soy sauce
    - 4 cloves roasted garlic, mashed
- **For the toppings:**
    - 1/4 cup bean sprouts
    - 1 tbsp fried garlic chips
    - 1/4 cup sliced green onions
    - Ramen noodles

Instructions:

1. **Prepare the broth:** Simmer stock with miso, soy sauce, and roasted garlic for **15 minutes**.
2. **Prepare the noodles:** Cook and drain ramen noodles.
3. **Assemble the ramen:** Pour broth over noodles, add toppings, and garnish with garlic chips.

Ramen with Tempura Shrimp

(A crunchy shrimp tempura ramen)

Ingredients:

- **For the broth:**
    - 4 cups dashi or chicken stock
    - 1 tbsp soy sauce
    - 1 tbsp mirin
- **For the toppings:**
    - 2 pieces shrimp tempura
    - 1/4 cup sliced green onions
    - 1 sheet nori
    - Ramen noodles

Instructions:

1. **Prepare the broth:** Simmer stock with soy sauce and mirin for **10 minutes**.
2. **Prepare the noodles:** Cook and drain ramen noodles.
3. **Assemble the ramen:** Pour broth over noodles, add tempura shrimp, and top with green onions.

Ramen with Kimchi and Pork Belly

(A tangy, spicy, and rich ramen with fermented flavors)

Ingredients:

- **For the broth:**
    - 4 cups chicken stock
    - 2 tbsp kimchi juice
    - 1 tbsp soy sauce
    - 1/2 tsp gochujang
- **For the toppings:**
    - 1/2 cup chopped kimchi
    - 2 slices pork belly (grilled or seared)
    - 1 soft-boiled egg
    - Ramen noodles

Instructions:

1. **Prepare the broth:** Simmer stock with kimchi juice, soy sauce, and gochujang for **10 minutes**.
2. **Prepare the noodles:** Cook and drain ramen noodles.
3. **Assemble the ramen:** Pour broth over noodles and add kimchi, pork belly, and egg.

Black Garlic Ramen

(A deep, complex ramen with caramelized garlic flavor)

Ingredients:

- **For the broth:**
    - 4 cups chicken stock
    - 2 tbsp black garlic paste
    - 1 tbsp soy sauce
- **For the toppings:**
    - 1 tbsp fried garlic chips
    - 1/4 cup sliced green onions
    - 1 soft-boiled egg
    - Ramen noodles

Instructions:

1. **Prepare the broth:** Simmer stock with black garlic paste and soy sauce for **15 minutes**.
2. **Prepare the noodles:** Cook and drain ramen noodles.
3. **Assemble the ramen:** Pour broth over noodles and top with fried garlic and green onions.

Ramen with Tsukune (Chicken Meatballs)

(A ramen featuring juicy chicken meatballs)

Ingredients:

- **For the broth:**
    - 4 cups chicken stock
    - 1 tbsp soy sauce
    - 1 tbsp mirin
- **For the meatballs (tsukune):**
    - 1/2 lb ground chicken
    - 1 tbsp soy sauce
    - 1 clove garlic, minced
    - 1 tsp ginger, minced
- **For the toppings:**
    - 1/4 cup chopped green onions
    - 1 soft-boiled egg
    - Ramen noodles

Instructions:

1. **Prepare the broth:** Simmer chicken stock with soy sauce and mirin.
2. **Make the tsukune:** Mix ground chicken with garlic, ginger, and soy sauce. Form small meatballs and cook in the broth.
3. **Prepare the noodles:** Cook and drain ramen noodles.
4. **Assemble the ramen:** Pour broth over noodles and top with tsukune and green onions.

Ramen with Fried Tofu

(A crispy tofu-topped ramen for a delicious vegetarian option)

Ingredients:

- **For the broth:**
    - 4 cups vegetable or miso broth
    - 1 tbsp soy sauce
    - 1 tbsp mirin
- **For the toppings:**
    - 1/2 cup firm tofu (cubed and deep-fried)
    - 1/4 cup sliced green onions
    - 1 soft-boiled egg (optional)
    - Ramen noodles

Instructions:

1. **Prepare the broth:** Simmer vegetable broth with soy sauce and mirin for **10 minutes**.
2. **Prepare the tofu:** Deep-fry tofu cubes until golden brown.
3. **Prepare the noodles:** Cook and drain ramen noodles.
4. **Assemble the ramen:** Pour broth over noodles, top with crispy tofu and green onions.

Ramen with Sweet Soy Sauce

(A ramen with a touch of sweetness for balance)

Ingredients:

- **For the broth:**
    - 4 cups chicken or vegetable broth
    - 2 tbsp soy sauce
    - 1 tbsp mirin
    - 1 tbsp brown sugar
- **For the toppings:**
    - 1/4 cup sliced bamboo shoots
    - 1/4 cup bean sprouts
    - 1 soft-boiled egg
    - Ramen noodles

Instructions:

1. **Prepare the broth:** Simmer broth with soy sauce, mirin, and brown sugar for **10 minutes**.
2. **Prepare the noodles:** Cook and drain ramen noodles.
3. **Assemble the ramen:** Pour broth over noodles, top with bamboo shoots and egg.

Ramen with Grilled Eel

(A rich, umami-packed ramen with unagi)

Ingredients:

- **For the broth:**
    - 4 cups dashi or chicken stock
    - 1 tbsp soy sauce
    - 1 tbsp mirin
- **For the toppings:**
    - 1 grilled eel fillet (unagi, sliced)
    - 1/4 cup sliced green onions
    - 1 soft-boiled egg
    - Ramen noodles

Instructions:

1. **Prepare the broth:** Simmer dashi with soy sauce and mirin for **10 minutes**.
2. **Prepare the noodles:** Cook and drain ramen noodles.
3. **Assemble the ramen:** Pour broth over noodles and top with grilled eel slices.

Ramen with Ramen Eggs (Ajitama)

(A simple ramen featuring perfectly marinated eggs)

Ingredients:

- **For the broth:**
    - 4 cups chicken stock
    - 1 tbsp soy sauce
    - 1 tbsp miso paste
- **For the toppings:**
    - 1 ramen egg (soft-boiled and marinated in soy sauce, mirin, and sugar)
    - 1/4 cup sliced green onions
    - Ramen noodles

Instructions:

1. **Prepare the broth:** Simmer stock with soy sauce and miso for **10 minutes**.
2. **Prepare the ramen eggs:** Soft-boil eggs, marinate in soy sauce, mirin, and sugar for **at least 4 hours**.
3. **Prepare the noodles:** Cook and drain ramen noodles.
4. **Assemble the ramen:** Pour broth over noodles and top with ramen egg.

Chili Crab Ramen

(A seafood ramen with a spicy crab sauce)

Ingredients:

- **For the broth:**
    - 4 cups seafood or chicken stock
    - 1 tbsp chili paste
    - 1 tbsp soy sauce
- **For the toppings:**
    - 1/2 cup cooked crab meat
    - 1 tbsp chili oil
    - 1/4 cup sliced green onions
    - Ramen noodles

Instructions:

1. **Prepare the broth:** Simmer stock with chili paste and soy sauce for **10 minutes**.
2. **Prepare the noodles:** Cook and drain ramen noodles.
3. **Assemble the ramen:** Pour broth over noodles, top with crab meat and drizzle with chili oil.

Pork and Gyoza Ramen

(A fusion ramen with pork and dumplings)

Ingredients:

- **For the broth:**
    - 4 cups tonkotsu broth
    - 1 tbsp soy sauce
- **For the toppings:**
    - 2 slices chashu pork
    - 3 pan-fried or steamed gyoza dumplings
    - 1/4 cup sliced green onions
    - Ramen noodles

Instructions:

1. **Prepare the broth:** Simmer tonkotsu broth with soy sauce for **10 minutes**.
2. **Prepare the noodles:** Cook and drain ramen noodles.
3. **Assemble the ramen:** Pour broth over noodles, top with pork and gyoza.

Sumo Ramen

(A hearty ramen packed with proteins and veggies)

Ingredients:

- **For the broth:**
    - 4 cups chicken or pork broth
    - 1 tbsp soy sauce
- **For the toppings:**
    - 1/4 cup ground pork
    - 1/4 cup cabbage
    - 1/4 cup mushrooms
    - 1/4 cup tofu cubes
    - Ramen noodles

Instructions:

1. **Prepare the broth:** Simmer stock with soy sauce for **10 minutes**.
2. **Cook the pork and vegetables:** Stir-fry ground pork, cabbage, and mushrooms.
3. **Prepare the noodles:** Cook and drain ramen noodles.
4. **Assemble the ramen:** Pour broth over noodles and add toppings.

Ramen with Sesame Paste

(A creamy, nutty sesame-based ramen)

Ingredients:

- **For the broth:**
    - 4 cups chicken stock
    - 2 tbsp sesame paste
    - 1 tbsp soy sauce
- **For the toppings:**
    - 1 tbsp toasted sesame seeds
    - 1/4 cup sliced green onions
    - Ramen noodles

Instructions:

1. **Prepare the broth:** Whisk sesame paste into stock with soy sauce, simmer for **10 minutes**.
2. **Prepare the noodles:** Cook and drain ramen noodles.
3. **Assemble the ramen:** Pour broth over noodles and sprinkle sesame seeds.

Ramen with Spinach

(A nutritious ramen with fresh spinach)

Ingredients:

- **For the broth:**
    - 4 cups miso broth
- **For the toppings:**
    - 1/2 cup fresh spinach
    - 1 soft-boiled egg
    - Ramen noodles

Instructions:

1. **Prepare the broth:** Simmer miso broth for **10 minutes**.
2. **Prepare the noodles:** Cook and drain ramen noodles.
3. **Assemble the ramen:** Pour broth over noodles, add spinach and egg.

Chicken Karaage Ramen

(A crispy chicken-topped ramen)

Ingredients:

- **For the broth:**
    - 4 cups chicken stock
    - 1 tbsp soy sauce
- **For the toppings:**
    - 2 pieces fried chicken karaage
    - 1 soft-boiled egg
    - Ramen noodles

Instructions:

1. **Prepare the broth:** Simmer stock with soy sauce for **10 minutes**.
2. **Prepare the noodles:** Cook and drain ramen noodles.
3. **Assemble the ramen:** Pour broth over noodles and top with karaage.

Ramen with Hot Sesame Oil

(A spicy sesame-infused ramen)

Ingredients:

- **For the broth:**
    - 4 cups chicken or vegetable broth
    - 1 tbsp sesame oil
    - 1 tbsp chili flakes
- **For the toppings:**
    - 1/4 cup sliced green onions
    - 1/4 cup bean sprouts
    - Ramen noodles

Instructions:

1. **Prepare the broth:** Simmer stock with sesame oil and chili flakes for **10 minutes**.
2. **Prepare the noodles:** Cook and drain ramen noodles.
3. **Assemble the ramen:** Pour broth over noodles and add toppings.

www.ingramcontent.com/pod-product-compliance
Lightning Source LLC
LaVergne TN
LVHW081319060526
838201LV00055B/2359